FLORENCE FOSTER JENKINS VOCAL / PIANO

ISBN 978-1-4950-7728-9

HAL•LEONARD®
7777 W. BLUEMOUND RD. P.O. BOX 13819 MILWAUKEE, WI 53213

For all works contained herein:
Unauthorized copying, arranging, adapting, recording, Internet posting, public performance,
or other distribution of the printed music in this publication is an infringement of copyright.
Infringers are liable under the law.

Visit Hal Leonard Online at
www.halleonard.com

Florence Foster Jenkins

By Alexandre Desplat

Moderate Swing

Copyright © 2016 SOLREY MUSIC
All Rights Administered by SONGS OF UNIVERSAL, INC.
All Rights Reserved   Used by Permission

When I Have Sung My Songs

Composed by Ernest Charles

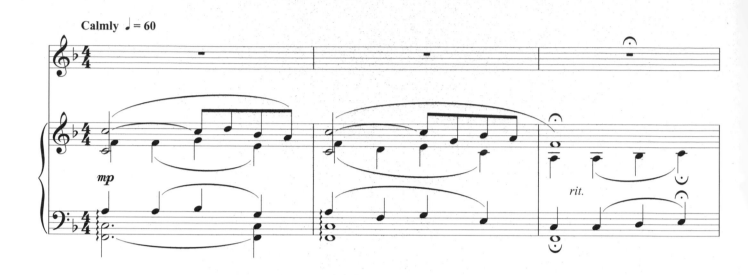

When I have sung my songs to you, _____ I'll sing no more.

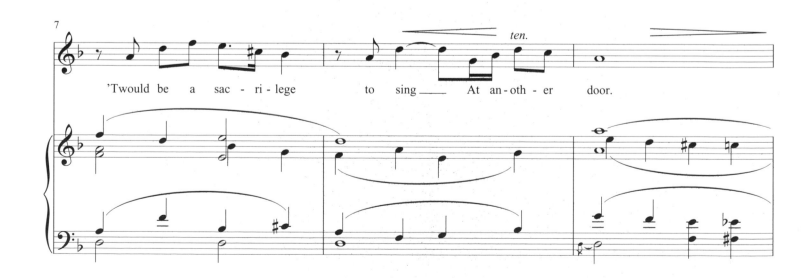

'Twould be a sac-ri-lege to sing ____ At an-oth-er door.

Copyright © 1934 (Renewed) by G. Schirmer, Inc. (ASCAP) New York, NY
International Copyright Secured   All Rights Reserved

Bribing

By Alexandre Desplat

Copyright © 2016 SOLREY MUSIC
All Rights Administered by SONGS OF UNIVERSAL, INC.
All Rights Reserved   Used by Permission

Socialite

By Alexandre Desplat

Copyright © 2016 SOLREY MUSIC
All Rights Administered by SONGS OF UNIVERSAL, INC.
All Rights Reserved   Used by Permission

Adele's Laughing Song

from *Die Fledermaus*

By Johann Strauss

Allegretto

O ___ no - ble sir, How ___ far you err! You're real - ly not ___ dis - creet; ___ There - fore my ad - vice Is that you look twice When judg - ing

Copyright © 2016 by HAL LEONARD LLC
International Copyright Secured   All Rights Reserved

O how fun - ny— ah, ha, ha! You a - muse me— ah, ha, ha! Ah,

ah, ah! Dear

Mar - quis, you are too ab - surd!

My pro - file's

Florence and Whitey

By Alexandre Desplat

Copyright © 2016 SOLREY MUSIC
All Rights Administered by SONGS OF UNIVERSAL, INC.
All Rights Reserved   Used by Permission

Slightly faster, steadily

molto rit.

McMoon

By Alexandre Desplat

Copyright © 2016 SOLREY MUSIC
All Rights Administered by SONGS OF UNIVERSAL, INC.
All Rights Reserved   Used by Permission

Sing Madame Florence

By Alexandre Desplat

Copyright © 2016 SOLREY MUSIC
All Rights Administered by SONGS OF UNIVERSAL, INC.
All Rights Reserved   Used by Permission

Prelude in E Minor
Op. 28, No. 4

By Frédéric Chopin

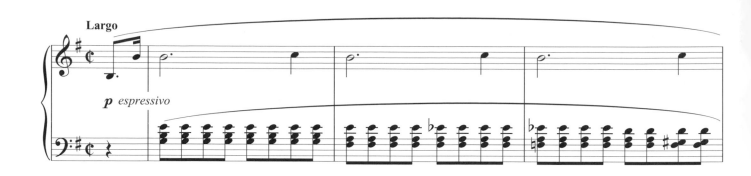

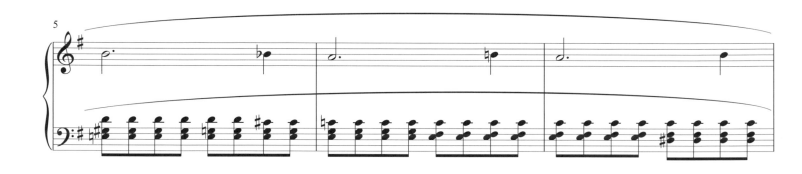

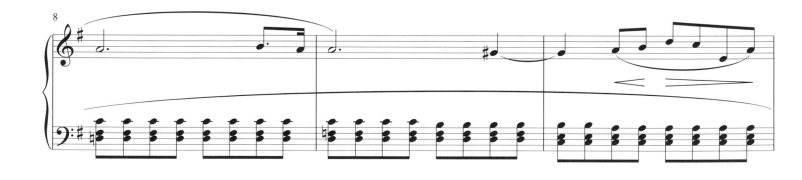

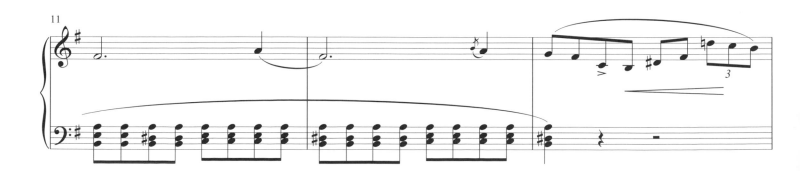

Copyright © 2016 by HAL LEONARD LLC
International Copyright Secured   All Rights Reserved

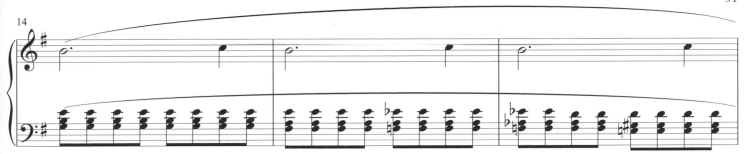

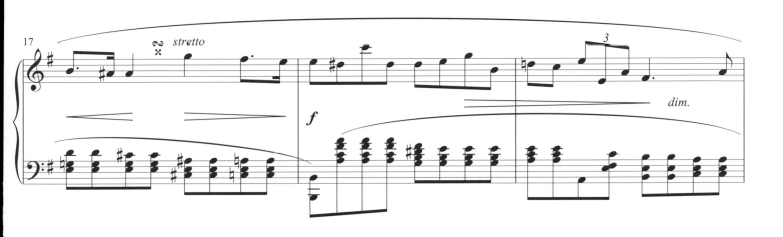

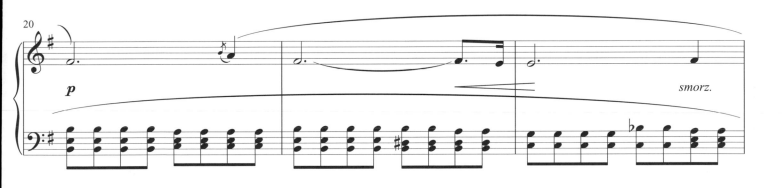

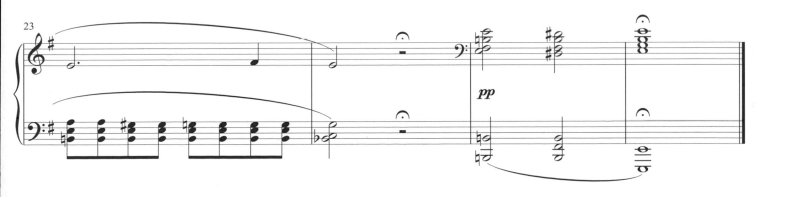

For Toscanini

By Alexandre Desplat

Copyright © 2016 SOLREY MUSIC
All Rights Administered by SONGS OF UNIVERSAL, INC.
All Rights Reserved   Used by Permission

Queen of the Night's Vengeance Aria
from *Die Zauberflöte*

By Wolfgang Amadeus Mozart

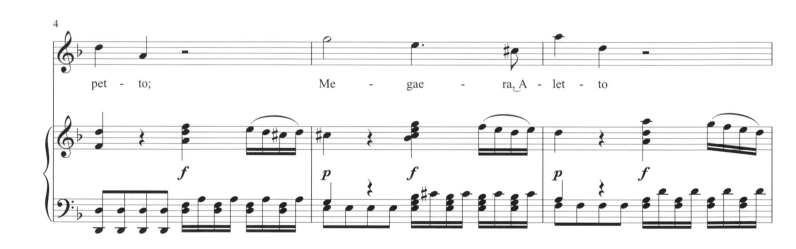

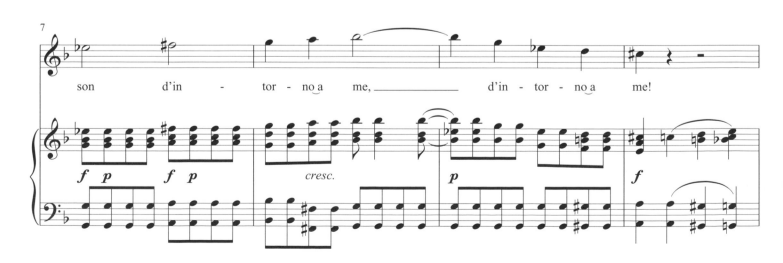

Copyright © 2016 by HAL LEONARD LLC
International Copyright Secured   All Rights Reserved

ser cru - del. Ti la - scio, ti

la - scio, t'ab - ban - do - no se non o - si es -

ser cru - del, es - ser cru -

del, _____

es - ser cru - del, es - ser cru -
del. Svel - ga al fel - lon, Pa - mi - na, svel - ga il

On Radio

By Alexandre Desplat

Moderately fast

Copyright © 2016 SOLREY MUSIC
All Rights Administered by SONGS OF UNIVERSAL, INC.
All Rights Reserved   Used by Permission

The Post

By Alexandre Desplat

Copyright © 2016 SOLREY MUSIC
All Rights Administered by SONGS OF UNIVERSAL, INC.
All Rights Reserved   Used by Permission

Indian Bell Song

from *Lakmé*

By Léo Delibes

This aria has been transposed down a whole step from the original key to match the key of the singer on the recording.

Copyright © 2016 by HAL LEONARD LLC
International Copyright Secured   All Rights Reserved

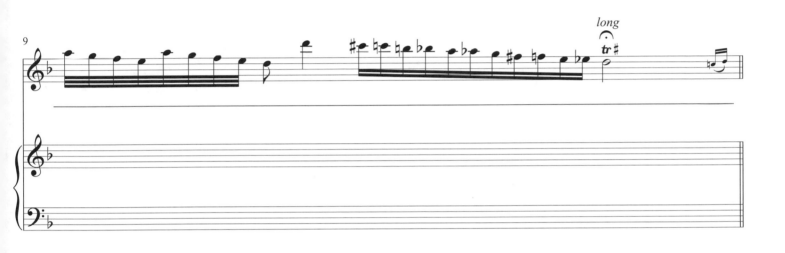

Andante *(presque en récitatif)*

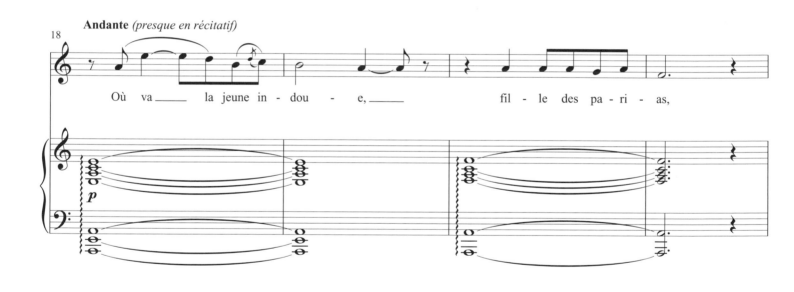

Où va____ la jeune in - dou - e,____ fil - le des pa - ri - as,

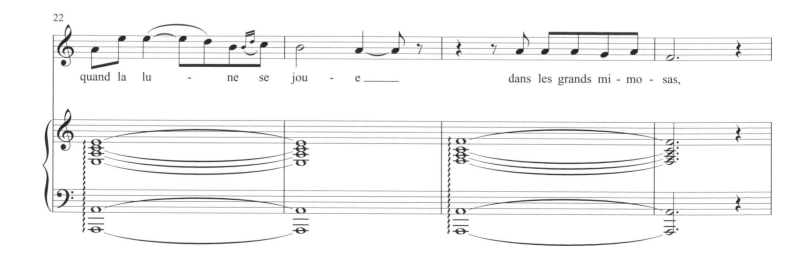

quand la lu - ne se jou - e ____ dans les grands mi - mo - sas,

le long des lau-riers ro - ses, rê-vant de dou-ces cho - ses,

ah! _____ el - le pas-se sans bruit et ri - ant à la

nuit, _____ à _____ la _ nuit! _____
(ah _____)

Là - bas dans la _ fo - rêt plus

* A cut has been made by the singer on the recording, reflected here.

Wiegenlied
(Lullaby)
Op. 49, No. 4

Words from 'Des Knaben Wunderhorn'
Music by Johannes Brahms

Zart bewegt

Gu - ten A - bend, gut Nacht, mit __
Gu - ten A - bend, gut Nacht, von __

Ro - sen be - dacht, ___ mit __ Näg - lein be - steckt schlupf __
Eng - lein be - wacht, ___ die __ zei - gen im ___ Traum dir __

un - ter die Deck: mor - gen früh, wenn Gott will, wirst du wie - der - ge -
Christ - kind - leins Baum: Schlaf nun se - lig und süß, schau im Traum's Pa - ra -

weckt, mor - gen früh, wenn Gott will, wirst du wir - der ge - weckt.
dies, schlaf nun se - lig und süß, schau im Traum's Pa - ra - dies.

This song has been transposed down a whole step form the original key to match the key of the singer on the recording.

Copyright © 2016 by HAL LEONARD LLC
International Copyright Secured   All Rights Reserved

The Swan
from *Carnival of the Animals*

By Camille Saint-Saëns

Copyright © 2016 by HAL LEONARD LLC
International Copyright Secured   All Rights Reserved